A PORTRAIT OF OLD JARROW

Volume 1

Paul Perry

S. B. Publications

Dedicated with thanks to my parents
Lucy and Albert Perry

First published in 1991 by S. B. Publications,
Unit 2, The Old Station Yard, Pipe Gate,
Market Drayton, Shropshire, TF9 4HY.

ISBN 1 870708 98 9

Typeset, printed and bound by
Manchester Free Press, Paragon Mill, Jersey Street, Manchester, M4 6FP.

CONTENTS

CONTENTS CONTINUED

Front Cover: Staple Road, Jarrow, c. 1920s.
Back Cover: The junction of Buddle Street and Commercial Road, 1953.
Title page: Invitation card for the launch of the battleship H.M.S. *Resolution* at Palmer's Shipbuilding yard, 11th May 1892.

ACKNOWLEDGEMENTS

The author is indebted to the following people without whom this book would not have been possible:

My wife, Kelly for her assistance and encouragement.

Special thanks to Joan Dale for her typing skill, patience and dedication to the project.

Sincere thanks to:-
Catherine Cookson for her letter of good wishes.
Janis Blower and the Shields Gazette.
Susan Mills — Curator of the Bede Monastery Museum.
Debra Turner.
Angela and Anthony Perry.
Robert and Eleanor Hare.
David Drynan.
Stephen Bell.
The Clergy of Jarrow.
Steve Benz for editing, publishing and marketing.

PREFACE

In 1966 I had 8 postcards of old Jarrow given to me by an old gentleman. The fascination I had for them urged me to fulfil my curiosity and find out how many more of these little gems were hidden away in shoe boxes in the attic. I appealed to the people of Jarrow to come forward, loan me what they had, and allow me to reproduce them and start a collection. It was difficult getting started — the hard part was to convince people their prints would come to no harm and would be returned as soon as negatives could be made.

Six months later I had about 30 prints, but not enough for an exhibition. My progress was slow, but I was prepared to continue the search. Many letters and phone calls later I managed to gain access to the archives at Durham and photograph their prints and maps, plus the co-operation from reference libraries and the South Shields Gazette. The collection was shaping up.

Exiled Jarrovians sent them from far and wide including Australia and America. At this point I got the feeling people were taking an interest and were looking forward to an exhibition. In October 1970 I was able to stage the eagerly awaited exhibition with 75 pictures more than 4 years after I first started collecting.

I have tried not only to collect the old Jarrow, but record the changing face of the town to the present day. Today the collection stands at 2000 photographs and in this book you will see a collection including Palmers shipyard, housing the birth of the Shopping Centre and a look at Jarrow through the eyes of James Hunter-Carr, a mushroom farmer and amateur photographer, who lived at Tyne Street. He recorded the town during the 30's, 40's and 50's compiling a detailed photographic record. It was my good fortune to inherit his collection and I take pleasure in sharing some of them with you.

I hope you gain as much enjoyment from this book as I have had compiling it.

Paul Perry

INTRODUCTION

There was a time when there was not a town called Jarrow — fields, streams and river banks were all that existed. Eventually settlements were raised in the area. Probably the most famous of the early settlements was an order of monks at the monastery at 'Donmouth' as it was referred to then. This was home to Jarrow's most celebrated resident, the Venerable Bede, monk, scholar and historian who was responsible for writing the oft referred to 'Northumbrian Chronicles' one of the few learned works to survive from those days. At that time Jarrow was a centre of learning, a beacon of light in a dark age. If all that Jarrow had to offer history was a monk and a book then it would still be worthy of note but Jarrow had more to give. The proximity of mineral resources and access to water borne transportation gave rise to the period of industrialisation which so dominated the life of the town from the eighteenth century to recent times. The shipyards and the steelworks, the coal mines, chemical plants and the oil tanks have all in their day played a role in the growth and wealth of the town.

When talking of Jarrow it is not always possible to talk about light and life, no work which ever purports in any way to tell the story of the town can ignore the hardship and privation suffered by its people during the inter-war years of the great depression. Subject to a greater rate of unemployment than any other borough in the land, Jarrow came to epitomise the unhappy state of affairs endured by much of industial Britain during that period. Nothing, depressions and wars included, lasts forever and the post war years saw a general improvement in the well-being of the town and its people. The improvement took many forms — new schools, public houses and clubs, a new shopping centre and, of course, the movement of many thousands of residents to Jarrow's own garden suberb, Primrose. There have been other changes too. In strict legal terms the Borough of Jarrow no longer exists, amalgamated as it was two decades ago into the new and much larger Borough of South Tyneside. The working base of the town has undergone equally radical alteration. Little of the heavy industry of old remains. Instead many would consider the borough to be a dormitory town, home to the office and shop personnel of the commercial enterprises of Newcastle and South Shields and to the wandering bands of construction and offshore workers. As someone once said "We are all travellers now'. Through the days of triumph and tragedy the outstanding feature of Jarrow has been its people. Famous writers, singers, local characters and villains, have grown up in the town but it is the ordinary Jarrovian possessing a rare mixture of honesty, decency and stoic good humour that has given the town its unique personality. In return, all are marked for ever by the town and have a genuine affection for it and pride in being 'Jarra Lads'.

So let us have one more glimpse down the years into the school yards and churches, the factories and the shops, the homes and the hospitals. Let us meet the men and women, our mothers and fathers perhaps, or even ourselves in younger days. You don't need your hat or your coat, you don't even need to leave your armchair, just turn the page and travel once more along the streets and down the back lanes of your town, my town, our town, Jarrow!

The Arms of the now defunct Borough of Jarrow symbolised the ancient association of the place with the Venerable Bede depicted by an open book and its connection through history with the sea with two sailing ships. An heraldic description reads:

Per Saltire Azure and Barry wavy of six Argent and of the first in Chief a Cross Flory of the second in fesse two Lymphads sails furled Or and in base an Open Book also of the second edged and Clasped Gold and inscribed with the words 'Beda Historia Ecclesiastica' Sable and for the crest Issuant from an Antique Crown Or a Demi'Dragon Azure Winged Vert holding between the claws a Crescent Gold.

Motto **"Labore et Scientia"**
The Latin Motto means **"Labour and Science"**.

St. John's Terrace This photograph was taken in 1955 at the junction of Ellison Street and William Street looking towards High Street. St. Bede's Church, which was consecrated in 1861, is in the centre. The town's medical practitioners had their surgeries in this elegant Victorian street. Now, the Probation Service have an office in the street.

Albert Road This photograph was taken in 1948 and shows the railway bridge on the main line between Newcastle and South Shields. The opening between McVitties shop on the right and the hoardings was known locally as the Giant Steps which led to Victor Street and on to Monkton Terrace.

For a street to be so called, it needs to have houses unlike a road or an avenue. Peel Street just qualified with only two houses. This street was more of a thoroughfare than anything else doing nothing more than connecting Ellison Street with Chapel Road. This photograph dates from 1935.

Ellison Street could have been termed the commercial side of the town, accommodating the banking facilities, Registrar's office and members of the legal profession. This picture, which was taken in the early part of the century, shows the Ben Lomond Hotel, re-named the Viking in the sixties, and the Longmore Fountain which was later moved to its present site in Springwell Park. Prior to 1881 the General Post Office was also situated in Ellison Street after which it was re-located in North Street.

Ellison Street showing Martins Bank which was incorporated into the Barclays Group in the late sixties. Next door was Tweddells Chemist shop. Further down the street was Shepherds, a department store which had the privilege of operating its own unique in-store currency, locally known as 'Shepherds money'. These odd shaped coins had the same value as coin of the Realm but could only be used at branches of Shepherds of Gateshead. Above this store was a billiard hall with 28 full size tables for hire by the half hour. This establishment was popular with men of all ages until its closure in the late fifties.

The Mechanics Institute also in Ellison Street was provided by Sir Charles Mark Palmer for the use of the community. It was to be used for social gatherings and reading rooms. This building boasted a comprehensive library which was also provided by Sir Charles at great expense to himself. Dance nights were always a popular attraction before and during the war years on Mondays and Fridays. In the early fifties this was taken over by Jarrow Council, renovated and re-named the Civic Hall and used for various functions. It could also be hired by the townsfolk for wedding receptions and the like. This photograph dates from around 1930.

Grange Road on what seems like a windy day taken from the corner of Ellison Street Masonic Hall to the left of the picture — taken in 1945. The Town Hall has stood majestically since it was opened by the town's first Mayor Sir Charles Mark Palmer in 1902. Notice the absence of the clock which wasn't erected until 1951, at a cost of £1000 bought with the balance of the Sir John Jarvis fund. This fund was supplied by the people of Surrey in 1935 where Sir John was a member of Parliament and High Sheriff. A public park in the town was named in his honour.

The 'Kino', latterly the Regal, one of Jarrow's three cinemas was in Grange Road. Patrons of the 'flea pit' as it was commonly known would queue from 5.30p.m. for the first house at 6 o'clock with a second performance at 8 p.m. Cinemas in those days did a roaring trade with a programme change every three days. This was one of the major leisure pursuits in the pre-television days. This photograph dates from 1953.

Grange Road pictured from Buddle Street showing the Gasworkers Club owned by the Mullen family and a forerunner of the Neon Club. To the right of the picture is the Ex-Servicemen's Club which was later moved to its present position in North Street. Nestled in the centre of the picture is the Regal, one of the town's three cinemas when this photograph was taken in 1955.

On the corner of Grange Road and Staple Road was the Royal Oak Hotel, better known as the 'Long Bar' owned by Kitty Monroe. When this photograph was taken in 1952 Kitty's, as it was also known, was a popular haunt for people of Irish descent, especially St. Patrick's day when one had to be there early in order to get a seat for the traditional ceilidh.

This photograph of **Staple Road** was taken in 1954 by James Hunter-Carr. To the left is the entrance to what once was Dunn Street school. Opposite was a pawnbrokers owned by a Mr. Hopper, who was one of the town's first Labour Councillors. Lamb's Potato Crisp factory had their warehouse in this cobbled street along with the Co-op. fruit and veg. dept. and Mrs. Risi's ice cream shop. Trams provided public transport until 1929 and the course of the old tramlines can be clearly seen.

The town had a wealth of corner shops. Practically every street in Jarrow had its own dimly-lit emporium where one could purchase anything from a gas mantle to a clay pipe. Many of these shops were open until midnight, some people spending and others just catching up on the latest gossip. Shanahans on the corner of Dee Street, Shearers in Wear Street, each had its own little army of customers. This photograph of Buddle Street in 1952 shows Mrs. Hawthorns shop. Further down the street lived a gentleman affectionately known as Johnny Lump – so called because of the shape of his nose – who owned a smokery producing kippers which his wife would sell door to door from a creel at 1d per pair often working from dawn to dusk.

This photograph showing Commercial Road in the background was taken from Ferry Street in 1952. Just visible is the garage of R. Houghton one of the town's three funeral directors the others being Burlison and Hedley of James Street and Western Road respectively.

Ferry Street photographed by James Hunter Carr in 1954 showing Frasers Glass Merchants to the right which is now the site of the Tyne Tunnel ventilator. On the left of the picture is the Golden Fleece just one of the town's 28 public houses. In the centre are the houses in Chaytor Street and beyond them is a view across the River Tyne of Howdon.

St. Peter's Church in Chaytor Street once boasted a steeple until a barrage balloon broke free from its moorings in the gas yard, which was alongside the church, and demolished it during the war years. Steps were taken to repair the steeple to its former glory but was found to be too costly. The decision was made to level it off and it remained this way until the church was demolished in the 60s. The church hall is on the left of this photograph taken in 1959 by James Hunter-Carr.

Jarrow School Board not only made education compulsory up to the age of thirteen, but initiated the first Board School, the Grange Board School, in the country. This was completed in 1873. The Church schools were being constructed after the new Education Act of 1870 by the Rector of Jarrow, Rev. Albert Ormsby, a keen educationalist and sensitive to the needs of the community. A site was selected in Chaytor Street and on 13th April 1874 the school opened and was called St. Paul's National School. At the turn of the century it was re-named St. Peter's. This photograph was taken in 1950 by James Hunter-Carr.

Pitt Street The building to the left was commonly referred to as the 'Rag Shop' where the individual could 'weigh in' disused clothing for a few coppers from Johnny Devlin during the 1920s. In 1935 a Mr. Towb bought the business from Devlin and renamed it Jarrow Iron and Metal Co. – but the name 'Rag Shop' stuck until its closure in the sixties. Totters came from all corners to bargain with the "Terrible Towb" in order to get the best possible prices for their day's collection of rags, worn out mangles and bedsteads. In the centre of the picture are the terraced houses in Buddle Street. The boarded up shop on the right was Mallens newsagency and general dealers before they moved to larger premises in Drury Lane. This picture was taken in the 1940s.

Market Square showing the Theatre Royal and Co-op. buildings. The theatre was built around 1850 and demolished in 1962 to make way for a housing complex. The Council, whose responsibility it was, were quoted £16,000 for the demolition work. Realising this figure was out of the question they decided to employ a Mr. Harry Hymers who was to do the job for £600. The rubble which resulted went on to form the base of the Lindisfarne roundabout at Primrose. Quite close to the Market Square was a private club called the Excelsior which later became Labour Party Headquarters before their premises in Park Road. Strakers butchers, clearly visible on the corner of Grange Road, would offer parcels of meat for 6d on a Saturday in the days before refrigerators. This photograph was taken from the remains of Burns Street in 1960 and I am grateful to the lady who donated it, whose name escapes me.

This picture of **North Street** was taken in 1947 by James Hunter-Carr. The Picture House, which is now a bingo and social club, is on the left. In the centre of the photograph is the Post Office which was opened on 2 August 1881. The two imposing white buildings were owned by Jarrow & Hebburn Co-operative Society. On the opposite side of the street was the entrance to Market Square, Carricks Bakers, a newsagents and Jimmy Campbell's second hand shop.

Shopping in Jarrow prior to the Arndale Centre was spread mainly over three streets, Ormonde Street, Grange Road and Monkton Road. The major shops seemed to be together in Ormonde Street - Burtons, Woolworths, the Benefit Shoe Co. to mention a few. These chain stores were supported on either side by the small trader, such as Burn's confectioners and Sheldon's the bakers opposite the printing works of the Jarrow Express, the town's very own newspaper until its closure in the early part of the century. This photograph dates from 1900.

This chain driven road roller is seen here in 1919 outside Pattersons fruit shop in Ormonde Street. At the wheel is Alfred Pearson who operated this vehicle for the Corporation for many years. It rattled and rolled its way through the streets at a snail's pace to various parts of the town undergoing road repairs where damage had been caused by the solid wheels of the many horse drawn vehicles of the time.

Halfway down Ormonde Street, next to Liptons grocer shop, there was an archway giving access to the rear of the street. In this arch sat a little old lady selling second hand clothes for a few coppers, barely making enough to make ends meet. She was there in all weather week in and week out for many many years, during the dark days of the depression in the thirties, through the war years until the fifties. Somewhere at the other end of this arch were a set of double doors reputed to be the entrance of the original Jarrow Market where much trading went on, possibly not all of it legitimate.

The Tram Service operated from the tram sheds at Tyne Dock to the terminus at Western Road from 1906 until it made way for the motor bus in 1929. These blue buses, with their hard wheels, provided the town with a regular service which was owned by a Mr. Charlton until bought by Northern General Transport. Picture taken 1922.

Junction of **Western Road and Wear Street** showing the premises of Radiant fireplaces in this photograph from 1955. Prior to this, the building was owned by W & J Hedley a firm of undertakers who loaned their horses to the Fire and Ambulance services as and when required. To the left of the picture is a Public House called 'the Queens'. Some years later this was re-named The Jarrow Lad. Opposite was another Public House 'The Rolling Mill' so named because it stands on what was once the Rolling Mills of the Palmer Shipyard, later the Consett Iron Company which ceased to trade in Jarrow in the 80s.

Councillors, local dignitaries and towns folk listen intently to the words of Councillor Violet Hope as she unveils a sculpture of two **Vikings** by C M. Davidson of Orpington, Kent on 19 February 1962. The statues were donated by Chippendale & Co., who built the shopping centre, to commemorate two invasions of Jarrow or Gyrwy as it was then called in the years 794 and 870.

Tyne Street, so called because of its proximity with the river. This photograph was taken in 1948 by James Hunter Carr and shows to the right of the picture more evidence of the size of the Palmer works. To the left is the house where bachelor Hunter-Carr lived and worked, tending his mushroom farm and writing music sadly none of which has survived. When the propery was demolished in the 50s he became a resident of the Kent Hotel in Jesmond, Newcastle until his death in 1964.

Clayton Street – to the left of the picture is the Baptist Chapel opened in 1879. The smart building in the centre is the premises of Commercial Permanent Building Society offices in Grange Road West. Just visible halfway down the street is the off-licence of P. G. Ward & Co. This photograph was taken in the summer of 1950.

Palmer Memorial Hospital, built in 1870 in memory of his first wife, was maintained by the contributions of Sir Charles Palmer's work force for whose use it was designed and supplemented by an annual subscription from the company. In the grounds of the hospital a bronze statue of Sir Charles Palmer by Albert Toft was erected in 1904 at a cost of over £2000 paid for by the workmen to commemorate the life and work of the founder of the company of which they were so proud. The Cenotaph is on the right of this picture taken in 1940.

No matter wher you are in Jarrow the imposing spire of Christ Church is visible from just about everywhere. In 1863, prior to the building of the church, evening services took place in the schools and in 1868 the Rev. John Bee was appointed first Rector of the new parish of Jarrow Grange. In 1869 with the financial support of Sir Walter and Lady James the church was built and consecrated on 5th October of the same year. The tower and spire with six bells were added to the church in 1882. The Golden Jubilee was celebrated in November 1919 when Dr. Moule, Bishop of Durham, dedicated two additional bells to make a full peal of eight, as a memorial to those men who fell in the 1914-18 war. No fewer than 56 rectors and curates have served its parishoners to the present day. An interesting note from an extract of the Churchwarden's Statement for 1883 reads: 'Income £165.00 with just £20 deducted for a whole year's heating and lighting'.

Jarrow had a small population of Italians - Fionda, Rea, Coletta to name a few. These families provided the town with ice cream parlours and fish and chip shops. This picture taken in 1952 of Staple Road shows Mrs. Rosa Risi's ice cream parlour on the corner of Cambrian Street. Because of the relationship between the Italians and Germans during the war years these parlours became targets for vandals. On four occasions Mrs. Risi replaced the windows of her shop; on the fifth she decided to board them up and they remained this way until the property was demolished in 1958. Similar misfortunes happened to the two families of German pork butchers in the town, Messrs. Abel and Egner.

Monkton Road had a wide variety of shops where one could purchase a 'stottie' from the Co-op., a ha'porth of snuff from Mrs. Antrobus or a piece of leather from Mr. Winchester to cobble your boots who would also charge up accumulators - a type of battery - to power the wireless, if you were lucky enough to own one. This photograph was taken in 1949.

This photograph of **Walter Street** was taken in 1950 and shows the County Hotel on the right. Just visible further down the street are the Public Baths which were opened in 1911. These premises were used by the community for swimming instruction and bathing for those with homes not fortunate enough to have adequate washing facilities which numbered many until the 50s. This building doubled as a dance hall when the swimming pool was covered with a specially made wooden surface and used as a dance floor. At the bottom of the street is the Golden Lion, a public house known locally as 'Johnnys' after the tenant John Inglis. In the centre of the picture are the ballast hills on the north side of the River Tyne at Howdon. These hills were composed of the waste ballast brought in on the empty oil and cargo ships, returning to the river. This ballast was used as a stabiliser in the early days of shipping.

Bede Burn Road with Christ Church steeple in the background. This was the main thoroughfare for public transport and still is today. A one-way system was introduced in the 1970s where this photograph was taken from in 1950. London and Newcastle Tea Company is on the right of the photograph, Reavley's Lemonade lorry is on the left. The area behind the bus in the centre of the picture is the junction of Albert Road and Humbert Street known locally as 'Carricks Corner'.

Pit Heap This was the site of the old Temple Pit, hence its name. Powells show people came to Jarrow with their travelling shows every year. To the right of the picture is the Prince of Wales Public House before it was demolished and re-built at the top of York Avenue. Corner shops were in abundance when this photograph was taken in 1955; the one in the centre of the picture was owned by Mallen who later became a wholesale tobacconist. The Tyne Tunnel ventilator now stands in this area.

These rare photographs of York Street were taken during the severe winter of 1947. Conditions became worse by the day as the snow came and the big freeze set in. Strong winds caused the snow to drift as high as six feet in places. The Council, unable to cope, hired snow ploughs to deal with the crisis.

While the adverse weather conditions worsened, Army vehicles were used to transport people to and from their place of work and assist in the moving of the growing mountain of drifting snow. Many of the elderly were confined to their homes for weeks relying upon friends and neighbours for food and warmth. Life was made more miserable due to various items still being rationed – coal, food and clothes among them.

Grant Street and the railway station. This rail link between Pelaw and South Shields was opened on 1 March 1872. The previous railway was from a junction near the present metro station at Pelaw down the mineral line, through Monkton Village, with a station in Jarrow near Wylam Street. This accounts for the unusual direction of Wylam Street from the rectangular street plan around it. Photograph taken in 1950.

The tranquility of **Park Road** is evident here in this photograph taken just before the turn of the Century. To the right of the picture is the Chapel of the Good Shepherd. Industry was never far away wherever you were in Jarrow. Visible to the left are the giant chimneys of Palmers Shipyard; most of the houses in the centre were owned by local businessmen - Andrew Pattie, Butcher, with retail premises in Ormonde Street and Terence O'Connor, a well known Grocer. This scene is much the same today with the exception of the chimneys which disappeared in the 30s and the disused Church was demolished in the 70s to make way for housing.

Monkton Terrace showing humpback bridge over the Newcastle to South Shields railway line. Whilst this bridge remains much the same today, the cottages have disappeared and have been replaced with more modern housing and sheltered accommodation for the elderly. On the other side of the bridge the terraced houses and corner shops have made way for a further housing development and the Tyne Tunnel approach road. This photograph dates from 1945.

Black & White Scratch Bands were fashionable in those bygone days when Jarrow came alive with its many carnivals during the 20s, 30s and 40s. The "Jarrow Savages" kept a smile on everyone's face with their antics during the dark days of the depression, along with the "Pirate" band from the Forresters Arms or the "Red Wine Shop" as it was commonly known. The most famous band of them all was the "King Tuts". These men were flamboyantly dressed as Arab princes and would entertain many hundreds of people as the carnival wound its way along the cobbled streets from the West Park where it commenced, led by those excellent musicians of Palmer's Band. Medals and cups were awarded for the originality of the many tableaux. Dancing and band competitions concluded the entertainment on the pit heap. This photograph is from 1929 and was taken in the grounds of the Ellison School.

Dunn Street School off Staple Road was severely bombed during the Second World War and this pre-fab. was all that remained of the school until it was demolished in the mid 60s. It was used as an annexe of St. Peter's Church of England School for such activities as fretwork and woodwork for the boys, with cookery lessons and domestic science for the girls demonstrated by a Miss Hallis.

This photograph was taken from the remains of the cobbled Stead Street in 1955.

Monkton Village before the turn of the century. The Lord Nelson Public House is to the right of the picture. This was converted from a cottage in 1834 and was taken over by a brewery in 1890. This building was demolished around 1930, rebuilt and remains largely unchanged today. In the centre of the photograph are Elmfield Cottages which are now part of the hospital.

The Durastic Company shown here in High Street where bitumen was manufactured until the late 50s; this substance was used to make buildings watertight when used in conjunction with roofing felt. On the horizon we see the 'slag heap' at Monkton which was composed of the waste deposits from the blast furnaces at Palmer's Shipyard. This was tipped from containers like molten lava and would illuminate he night sky and was visible many miles away. The task of moving this mountain of clinker was, in itself, a full time occupation which started in the 30s and was still being moved into the 70s. Perhaps this will illustrate the enormous quantities of steel produced. The slag which was removed was used as hard core for the many roads in the region under construction before and after the Second World War. Lorries came from as far as Nottingham and the west coast for a plentiful supply of this material. This photograph dates from 1950.

The Union flag, bunting and banners display the excitement of wives, mothers and children as they celebrate the end of the 1914–18 war and await the safe return of their loved ones with a street party in **Nansen Street**. Another classic example of the community spirit which Jarrow had in abundance.

The Paper Mill was owned by the Richardsons, a family of land and property owners who resided in Monkton Lodge opposite the Mill. After Mr. Richardson's sudden death in 1923 his widow sold the mill to another family of substance called Scott who lived at Monkton Hall - which is now a hospital in the village. They turned the lodge into a prosperous nursery business and leased part of the mill to the Council who operated the Jarrow Instruction Centre from the early 30s. This was for the benefit of the growing numbers of unemployed and gave them tuition in furniture making, history, geography, a host of other subjects and sporting activities. After Mr. Scott's death in 1947 the lodge was bought by a family of seed merchants called Gregory. Today this house, overlooking Springwell Park, is a rest home for the elderly and the old mill is now the property of Kenton Utilities.

The President of the Board of Trade, Sir Stafford Cripps, K.C., M.P., visits the Bede Trading estate on 10th December 1946. He is pictured here with the Mayor of Jarrow Alderman J. Hanlon and Mayor of South Shields Alderman R. Longstaffe. It was a visit of Sir Stafford in September 1945 that resulted in the inauguration of the Bede Trading Estate development. 1945 also saw the election of Right Honourable Ellen Wilkinson, M.A., as the town's Member of Parliament. She was later to become Minister for Education.

Jarrow. M.P. Ellen Wilkinson inspects the new **Bede Trading Estate** in 1948 which attracted many major companies to the town - Paton & Baldwins, Morganite Resistors and the Cigarette Components Ltd. among them. With her is Councillor Joe Simonds a self-educated man and stalwart of the Labour movement in Jarrow who travelled Europe with his knowledge of Municipal housing. Also pictured are the Town Clerk, Mr. Perkins, Alderman Rose and Councillor Morrison.

Curlew Road This photograph was taken from the gasometer in 1956 and shows new Council housing being erected in the Queen's Road area. In the background are the remains of Stead Street cottages and beyond, the taller houses of High Street. The foreground shows a penned area; this was for the manufacture of breeze blocks - a type of brick - for the building industry. Close to this was Jarrow Cricket Club and pitches, the headquarters of the Sea Cadets, Lamb's blacksmiths shop and an acetylene gas works which was the victim of a major explosion in 1928.

The Mercantile Dry Dock was opened on 21 August 1889 with three dry docks and a full order book. To the right of the picture is the fitting shop and left is number 3 dock, a fourth dock was to be built in 1956. In the background is the property of Shell Mex and B.P. Ltd. and beyond this was the area called 'the Slake'. This word was a corruption of the term Jarrow's lake. Close to the slake was a floating quarantine hospital owned by Port of Tyne Health Authority. During the 1930s ships entering the Tyne were obliged to fly a flag called the 'Yellow Jack' – this was to signify that the vessel had come from foreign parts. This photograph dates from 1948.

In 1851 Sir Charles Mark Palmer, in conjunction with his brother George, commenced the business of shipbuilding under the name of Palmer Brothers & Co. It was a modest beginning like many other businesses founded in that decade. The day of wooden ships had not passed but the Palmer brothers saw that it was coming to a close.

ARRIVAL OF IRON SCREW COLLIER,
"JOHN BOWES,"
IN THE COLLIER DOCK OF THE EAST AND WEST INDIA DOCK RAILWAY, LONDON,
AUGUST, 1852.

Their first vessel in 1851 was a mere tug boat but it wasn't long before the brothers went on to greater things. In 1852 the John Bowes was launched. This vessel had the privilege of being the first iron screw collier. After a remarkably long life of eighty two years in service, she ran aground on the Northern coast of Spain and was broken up under the name of 'Valentin Fierro'.

The Palmer success story was aided with the use of a steel rolling process, rather than the forged method. The yard housed eight miles of internal railway and boasted the biggest foundry on the East coast.

An impressive galvanizing plant said to be the largest and busiest in the country, as were the unique German built cantilevered overhead cranes which towered above the yard's 140 acres and indeed the whole of Jarrow. It had long been the boast of Jarrovians "at Palmers they take in iron ore at one end of the works and turn it out again in the shape of a ship at the other".

H.M.S. *York* was launched by H.R.H. The Duchess of York, latterly Queen Elizabeth the Queen Mother, on 15th July 1928. On the same day, Her Majesty officially opened York Avenue.

These works were among the biggest of their kind and employed best part of the town's male working population. No fewer than nine hundred ships were launched at Palmers until its gates finally closed in 1933. Pictured - the Boiler House in 1912.

Sir Charles died in 1907 and was buried in North Yorkshire on 7th June.

On 4th June 1947 the Minister of Transport, the Right Hon. Alfred Barnes M.P., inaugurated the Tyne Pedestrian Tunnel works. Work commenced at Jarrow and at Howdon on the north bank simultaneously with the aim of meeting in the middle.

The work went well and breakthrough was right on target and ahead of schedule ninety feet beneath the river. Two tunnels, each 300 yards in length, one each for pedestrians and cyclists, were built at a cost of £750,000. Entry to and exit from the tunnels was by escalator. At the time of construction, these moving staircases were the longest in the world at 186 feet in length. Elevators were provided for the use of wheelchairs and perambulators. The complex was completed in 1951 and officially opened in 1952.

In October 1936, led by Ellen Wilkinson, 200 hungry men desperate for work marched 276 miles to London carrying with them a petition of 10,000 signatures. This was to be presented to Downing Street to make the Government aware of the unemployment situation not only in Jarrow ut the North East in general. This photograph of the marchers shows them in one of their makeshift shelters enjoying a joke and a welcome meal of broth. The hearts of the nation went out to these proud men from Jarrow 'The Town that was murdered' who were fighting for their town, their right to work and for future generations. The men were overwhelmed by the kindness shown to them every step of the way. Footsore and weary they were offered food and accommodation in church halls and community centres during the three weeks it took to complete their crusade.

This photograph of the railway bridge over Albert Road was taken during the summer of 1928 and shows the aftermath of a storm which lasted just ten minutes. Hailstones as big as golf balls were reported to have fallen, breaking windows and causing extensive damage to roofing and chimney stacks. On contact with the ground the hailstones fused together creating huge blocks of ice, making conditions hazardous for those on foot and horse drawn vehicles. The floods that followed brought with them further problems.

This backyard in Albion Street is further evidence of the conditions in which some of the townsfolk lived. The stairway to the upper flat was demolished because of the dangerous condition resulting from lack of maintenance and was replaced with a makeshift ladder. Geese and chickens roaming freely scratching for something to eat were a common sight in most backyards in Jarrow. These were kept mainly for the eggs they provided which were in short supply commercially during the lean times of the 1920s when this photograph was taken. Almost every home in Jarrow had a cat or dog, sometimes both, to control the vermin.

This photograph was taken in 1935 and shows unemployed shipyard workers at the Jarrow Institution Centre located at the disused papermill in Springwell Road, making what was to become known as the 'Bede Table'. This was made from solid oak donated by the Dean of Westminster, Reverend Prebend Austin Thompson and bearing his coat of arms, St. Paul's crest with the words 'Sanctus Paulus' and the inscription of the dedication stone. The table is still in use today at St. Paul's Church. Various other items of furniture were made by these talented men for use at the Palmer hospital. Some were sold with the proceeds going towards the welfare of the centre.

The Jarrow school of physical culture and their coaches on September 9th 1908. This fine body of men in the peak of condition would train seven nights every week and were rewarded with the medals, cups and trophies they won in the many local and national boxing and weightlifting competitions.

These two horses, Peggy and Sandy, after twelve years of service with Jarrow Corporation Cleansing Department were to be retired to assist in agriculture on Dodds farm at Hedworth. These horses were popular with young and old, often stopping for an apple or the occasional carrot as they pulled the heavy dust carts through the streets of Jarrow until the mid 40s. Although reliable, this type of transportation, both costly and very slow, was soon to be replaced by motorised dust carts. Perhaps not as quaint as Peggy and Sandy but certainly more efficient.

This photograph of the Well at Bede Burn was taken in 1902 and shows St. Cuthbert's vicarage in the background. Whilst there is evidence that this well existed at the time of Bede, it is most unlikely that it was used by him or any other monk from the Bede Monastery. The river Don is tidal and in mediaeval times it contained fresh water which flowed alongside the monastery. It is believed the monks used this as their water source.

Today, East Jarrow is well known as being the birthplace of Catherine Cookson, O.B.E., M.A., world famous novelist and one of the country's most prolific writers whose stories, set in the North East, have been translated into many languages and enthralled the millions of fans she has gained throughout the world. This photograph was taken in 1975 and shows Catherine on one of her rare visits to Jarrow with the Church Committee at St. Peter's, York Avenue.

Straw boaters and Sunday best clothes were the order of the day for management and senior sales assistants of Robert Andison & Co. Wine and Spirit Merchants of North Street for their annual summer outing courtesy of the company. This party was probably part of a charabanc trip which were fashionable and very popular in the beginning of the century when this photograph was taken. Robert Andison & Co. were prominent in the town as mineral water manufacturers, supplying shops and breweries, in stone bottles and earthenware flagons similar to the one in this picture.

Just two of the town's fleet of ten dairymen Messrs. Pattinson and Scott pose for the camera with their offspring who were to follow in the footsteps of their forefathers and deliver the milk to those who could afford it. This photograph was taken in 1900.

The entrance to the recently opened Tyne Tunnel can be seen in the centre of this picture taken from Monastery Court in 1967. Beyond, clearly visible, is the approach road winding its way to meet the busy A19 two miles away. The Festival flats are on the right and the derelict remains of the houses in part of Salem Street immediately behind them.

Public Conveniences situated at the junction of High Street and Monkton Road. The houses in Burns Street are visible to the left of this photograph taken in 1948. Adjacent to this unusual looking building was what was known as the 'Old Man's Shed' a wooden structure for the use of retired gentlemen where they could meet, stoke up their pipes and swap yarns of yesteryear.

The traditional Mayor's Sunday Procession commenced from the Town Hall, through the streets of Jarrow. This yearly event, which drew huge crowds, took place upon the election of the Mayor of the town. This photograph was taken in June 1965 and shows his Worship the Mayor, Councillor Ralph C. Sparks with the Town Clerk Gerald T. Noon and members of the Council en route to St. Paul's Church for a thanksgiving service. Musical accompaniment was provided on these occasions by the bands of the Sea Cadets, Territorial and Salvation Armies. The building to the left is Jarrow Hall overlooking the Drewett Playing Fields.

The first sod was cut for Council housing in 1920 and the first house occupied in 1921. From then until the cessation of building in 1940 because of the war, 1740 houses were provided at Primrose at a cost of £890,000. Building re-started in 1945 and in 1963 the Council celebrated the opening of the 5,000th house. The town's M.P. Ellen Wilkinson, or 'Wee Ellen' as she was known, is seen here with Councillors Joe Symonds, Alderman Rennie, Sir. H. Stoddart and the Town Clerk, Mr. Perkins, inspecting the recently opened houses in Stanhope Road in 1946.

The next target on the Council's programme was the demolition and re-building of the Queen's Road area. At this time, in the 1950s when this photograph was taken, the accommodation in the town centre was of a very poor standard. Rat infested and overcrowded conditions were not uncommon. Many of these properties were blighted with severe dampness which was largely to blame for the poor state of health of many of the occupants.

This was to be followed by Palmer Street, Bladen Street and houses in the immediate vicinity, again these houses were to be demolished to make way for a modern style housing estate which was to become known as the Wear Street Development. This aerial photograph dates from 1963.

In 1952 the festival, or Coronation flats, became available; a complex of 84 dwellings, three storeys high. This was the first move towards slum clearance in the town centre. Sadly this type of house was a prime target for vandalism and despite a continual repair programme, the authorities decided to cut their losses and demolish them in 1982 after a life span of just thirty years.

B2 Phase two of the demolition. This time the hammer came down on Cambrian Street and Staple Road A sad end to what was once classed as luxury housing which were built ahead of their time.

In the early part of the sixties, a total of 641 houses had been completed in the town centre and this was before the construction of the multi-storey flats on the Market Square clearance site. Also at this time, further housing developments were in progress on the Hedworth Estate which was in the boundaries of Boldon Urban District. This was to provide a further 1,200 dwellings by Jarrow Council and became known as the 'overspill'.

This photograph of the Scotch Estate dates from 1958.

Before the turn of the Century a Byelaw introduced by the Corporation stated that no Public Houses were to be built on the southern side of the town, namely the area beyond the Railway Station in Grant Street. All such places were to be contained in and around the town centre with an exception for the major political parties, in order to keep this part of the town strictly residential. This photograph of the Station Stairs was taken in 1949.

Education facilities grew in the early 19th century along with the expanding industry and population. No photographic records exist of the town's first school, located on land between St. Paul's church and the monastery ruins. East Jarrow Roman Catholic school was opened in 1872 to meet the growing needs of the population at Low Jarrow. The staff comprised one headmistress, one pupil teacher and three monitors aged 13 who had to cope with a roll of 112. This photograph of the school was taken in the 1930s.

St. Bede's school class of 1928–29 standard 3C with teachers Miss Finnigan and Mr. Edmund McPeake.

Salt Grass situated behind St. Paul's Road. This area was once used for drying the salt brought in on sailing ships hence its name.. St. Paul's Church, to the left of the picture, is above the mineral line which terminated at the Shell Oil Terminal. Picture taken 1950.

This photograph was taken in 1896 and shows Hedworth Hall set in the trees and owned by market gardener Robert Jobling. After his death some time around 1930 his widow Dorothy moved to a house called 'The Dene' to the left of the picture, where she carried on the business of market gardening. The Hall, by this time in need of considerable repair, was purchased by Mary Harris in the early 30s. The barn at the foot of the picture was part of 'Mill Farm'. This location was to become known as 'Fisher's Dene' named after the owner of Mill Farm John Fisher. Although the road is still in use today, the buildings have long since disappeared.

The original Jarrow ferry 'The Dexter' pictured here at the landing at Jarrow, was built by Palmers and retired from service sometime in 1923. This photograph dates from 1910.

A. B. Gowan I was added to the Jarrow Ferry Service on 10 July 1921. This modern vessel was to work alongside the ageing paddle ferry built by Palmers. This service, which operated between Jarrow and Howdon on the north bank was for motor vehicles, cyclists, horse drawn carts, hand barrows and foot passengers. In later years it was used solely for vehicles due to the opening of the pedestriann tunnel in the 50s.

Councillors, dignitaries and their wives donned their Sunday best for a trip on board the latest addition to the ferry service, A. B. Gowan, during its trials on 10th July 1921. Mr. A. B. Gowan, a senior manager at Palmers where the ferry was built and whom it was named after, is seated in the centre of the picture.

Engine Room A. B. Gowan II John Suggitt engine man on the last run across the Tyne to Howdon in September 1967 when the service ceased to operate after the completion of the Tyne Tunnel in July 1967.

Hold it! said the cameraman to members of the **Jarrow Cycling Club** as they stand proud with their machines, complete with oil lamps, for this photograph taken in 1910 outside St. Bede's Parochial Hall and Institute in Chapel Road. This building was for leisure pursuits only in those days. The Church frowned upon alcoholic refreshment for these premises. Brothers of a Monastic order who taught in the local Catholic schools resided in this Church owned house just after the turn of the Century. The building was demolished in the 70s.

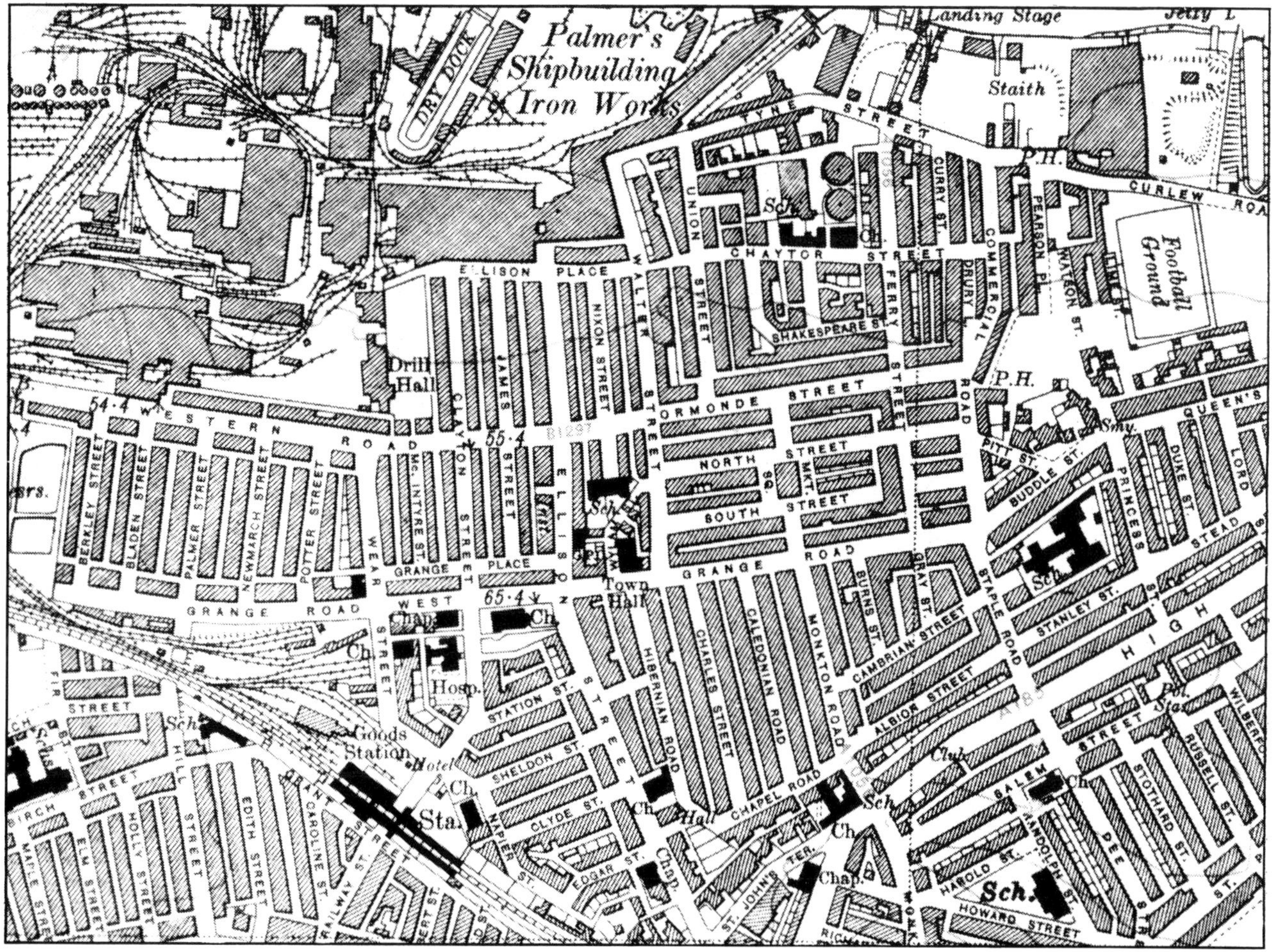

Street map of the central area of Jarrow. Much has changed since this map was published in 1930. Long gone are the terraced houses of Albion and Stead Street, as well as some of the many churches Jarrow once boasted which catered for the many denominations present in the town. Evident at the top right of the picture is the vast area of the Palmer shipyard which was to close later in this decade rendering many out of work.

(i) The 'Berengaria' pictured here moored alongside the now disused Palmer's quay in 1936. It was bought from Germany for scrap by Sir John Jarvis to provide work for the unemployed men of Jarrow. Their task was to remove the superstructure as far as main deck level. The elaborate furnishings of this former luxury liner were to be sold by auction prior to the operation. Visitors came from near and far to catch a glimpse of the luxurious fittings which adorned this queen of the sea, and perhaps take home a souvenir many of which are still in existence today. Local traders queued for hours to purchase the ornate bathroom suites, decorative wall panelling and carpeting which went on to grace the walls and floors of the well heeled.

Germany held the secret of making concrete as hard as steel, which was used to secure the prop shaft to the hull of the 'Berengaria'. Several attempts were made to blast the concrete but all to no avail. Eventually cracks appeared in the hull of the ship, which had to be repaired prior to it being towed to a breakers yard in Rosyth, Scotland to complete the task. The resulting scrap metal was to be sold back to Germany which was at this time going through a financial crisis. They offered in return for the scrap metal — which was much sought after — a steel tube rolling mill for Jarrow. Sir John and the Corporation welcomed this further lease of life for the town and the prospect of jobs for its many unemployed. A new industry was born and became known as the 'Tube Works'.

St. Bede's Church was consecrated and officially handed over, as a new parish for the Catholic community, to Father Meynell on 27th December 1861 in the presence of Bishop Hogarth. Prior to this, Mass was celebrated at a house in High Street by Father Edmund Kelly, a Priest from St. Bede's Church, South Shields who was responsible for the founding of the Jarrow Parish. No fewer than 59 Priests have resided and served Mass here since the Parish was founded in 1861. Two other Parishes were created in the town to cater for the growing numbers of Roman Catholics - St. Matthew's in 1935 and St. Mary's in 1952. This photograph dates from 1900.

St. Bede's Church had a choir when the parish was founded in 1861. Due to lack of choristers it was later dissolved but revived in 1962, thanks to Gerard McNally a teacher from St. Bede's school. He was responsible for the success the choir enjoyed which at its height boasted 40 boys and 20 men. During the 60s the choir was invited to join 'Pueri Cantores' an international choir organisation which translated means 'Boys Choir'. The National Church music Association offered an invitation in order to broaden their knowledge of music and give the choir the opportunity to visit and sing in different parts of the country. Their travels were later to take them to Holland, Germany, France, Belgium and Italy. On one occasion in 1967 in Rome one of the Jarrow boys, William Woodhouse, was chosen from many hundreds to sing before His Holiness Pope Paul VI who rewarded him with the presentation of a watch. This photograph was taken on the altar of St. Bede's Church in 1970.

As part of its plan for re-developing the town, the Council decided to develop a seven acre site in the central area for a major shopping centre complete with one hundred shops, parking for two hundred cars and a ten pin bowling centre. Councillors Violet Hope and Dennis McCluskey with officials from the Arndale Property Trust Co. viewing a model of the proposed centre. This photograph dates from 1957.

The site was chosen because it was conveniently near to both railway and bus stations. In the mid fifties the area had to be cleared to make way for this exciting new venture. The houses in Charles Street, Caledonian and Hibernian Roads had to be demolished. The Council decided the most economical way to do this was to burn them down. This mammoth task was undertaken and controlled by Durham County Fire Brigade.

One side of Grange Road was completely demolished which included many shops and public houses. The developers moved in and a new era of shopping was born. The centre attracted many big companies which had previously been established in Ormonde Street. the town's former shopping area. This photograph was taken in 1958.

In 1961 the first phase of thirty five shops was opened and people soon became accustomed to the new style of modern day shopping. Visitors came from far and wide to see one of the biggest traffic-free shopping precincts in the country. The development was designed on the pedestrian basis and to meet the requirements of the people of Jarrow and the surrounding areas, together a population of some 50,000.

This photograph was taken from the roof of Ellen Court in the mid 1960s. The area in the centre of the picture is now occupied by a ventilation shaft for the Tyne Tunnel. The two white buildings in the foreground were the premises of Jarrow and Hebburn Co-operative Society who had a department store in North Street and tea rooms close by in Market Square until 1960 when they moved to the Arndale Centre. One of the buildings was later to become the Cavalier Club bar and restaurant. To the left of the gasometer is the Commercial Hotel reputed to be the oldest public house in the town. The name was changed to the Tunnel Tavern in the 70s and later to its present name The Gaslight. Notice the absence of shipping in what was formerly a very busy stretch of the river Tyne. The 60s witnessed the decline and eventual closure of the shipbuilding and repair yards in this area.

Every junior school in the County had a football team and Jarrow was no exception – St. Peter's, the Ellison, the Grammar School – but none of these came up to the standard of the boys at **St. Bede's**. Their success was due to the efforts of their coaches, Hugh Cunningham and Ned Burke, two devoted teachers at St. Bede's. So good was their tuition the team went on to win the league cup and St. Oswald's Shield eight years in succession, a record surpassed by none. Also pictured in this team photo 1925–26 season are teachers Felix Sullivan, Sep. McAlarney and Pat Corr who went on to become head at St. Bede's.

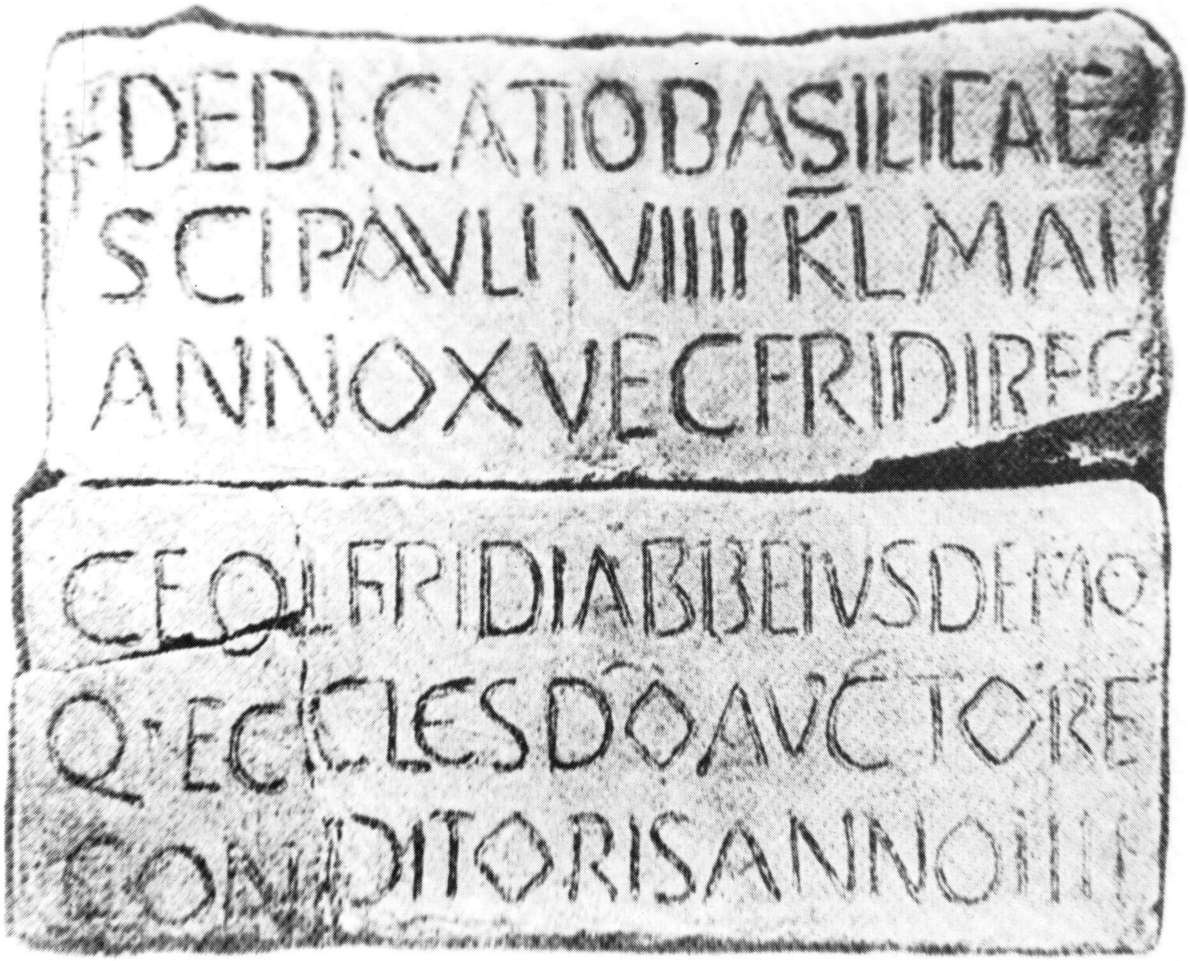

St. Paul's Church was dedicated in the year 685. The stone which commemorates this historic milestone is situated above the chancel arch and the translation reads:

The dedication of the church of St. Paul on the Ninth of the Kalends of May in the Fifteenth year of King Ecgfrith and the Fourth year of Coelfrith, Abbot and with God's help the founder of this church.

"I have spent my whole life in the same monastery and while attentive to the rule of my Order and the service of the Church, my constant pleasure lay in learning, teaching and writing." These words were said by Bede in the monastery he loved at Jarrow. Bede entered the monastery on the consecration of the Abbey in A.D.685 and remained there until his death in 735. A man of great learning he earned himself the enviable title of the Father of English learning.

In the year 1070 an army of William the Conquerer destroyed the original monastery by fire. It was rebuilt in 1075 but alas dissolved in 1540 and its ruins have lain next to St. Paul's church at the mouth of the Tyne close to the 'slake' for over 400 years. The word 'slake' is a corruption of the term Jarrow's lake.

Although it probably had a Roman occupation, the name Jarrow is derived from the Saxon word Gyrwy meaning marsh. It was also referred to as Jarrois in a print of the 'old church'
The town as it was then with a population of just 1,400 was invaded by the Danes in 794 A.D.

The Chancel at St. Paul's Church was founded in the year 681a.d. before the arrival of Bede. The basilica wasn't built until later in the decade and they were two separate structures not joined until the year 685a.d. with the tower as we know it today. At that time the population was few and poor, consisting mainly of farmers and fishermen on the Tyne. This would account for the neglect of the church structure which became unsafe forcing the demolition of the larger of the Saxon churches in 1782 and the erection of a poor substitute. In 1866 the present nave of the church was founded together with the north aisle.

Jarrow Hall was built between 1785 and 1800 by Simon Temple. It has many rooms including an oval room with a unique curved door. Simon Temple was born in 1759 in the village of Westoe, South Shields. His parents owned a small but prosperous shipbuilding business. In 1795 he acquired a substantial estate at Jarrow including St. Paul's Church and surrounding areas. In 1798 he opened a new dry dock at South Shields, at that time one of the most efficient in the country. On 26th September 1803 he opened the infamous Alfred Pit at Jarrow. After a grand and elaborate opening creating many jobs he started the industrial growth at Jarrow.

He was a caring employer and in 1804 he built rows of white walled miners cottages next to St. Paul's Church and on some high ground close by known today as High Street. These cottages remained until 1934 when they were demolished. Due to mismanagement his empire began to collapse around him; in 1806 failing mining investments and a shipyard at Dunkirk Place, Jarrow led to his bankruptcy. Temple died in 1822 aged 63 in the house of his ex-butler. A sad end to a great industrialist who contributed so much to the development of Jarrow. Today Jarrow Hall is the Bede Monastery Museum containing many artifacts from the ancient monastery near St. Paul's Church and has featured in many period dramas for television from the Catherine Cookson stories.

Drewett Ormonde Drewett was born in 1839 at Jarrow Hall and studied law at Oxford. In 1867 he adopted the surname Drewett and married Catherine Mary Burrell. In the same year he was elected as member of the local Board of Health for Jarrow and by 1872 was Chairman of the Board. He was generally involved in local Government through his concern for the welfare of the Jarrow population and was often at odds with his role as a local land and property owner. In 1895 he refused to give the town Council a site for an east end park though he was willing to lease the land for 21 years at a rent of £1 per acre per annum.

The Council could not agree to his proposals and decided to seek another site elsewhere. Drewett Ormonde Drewett passed away in March 1910. Having no children of his own he left his wealth and property to Alfred Henry Chaytor, a New Zealander adopted by the Drewetts. In 1911 Alfred Chaytor donated the field south of the Hall to create a park in memory of his adopted uncle. The Council accepted his donation and in 1912 the Drewett Playing Fields were officially opened at considerable expense to the rate payers. A park keeper, Charles Harrison, was appointed to maintain the standards laid down by Chaytor and it soon became known as 'Charlies Park' a name by which it is still known today.

Bandstand at Drewett Park. This photograph was taken in 1900. Notice the miners "White Cottages" on the left of the picture; to the right is St. Paul's Church.

Magistrates, Councillors and officials at the opening of the new Police Court Buildings, **Clervaux Terrace** on Monday 27th January 1930. The last 'County Court' sitting at Jarrow was on 6th December 1937.

In 1922 Jarrow had 28 public houses not to mention the workingmens clubs and to this day it is a well known fact quite a few hardened drinkers set out to have a pint in each one but there were not many who returned to boast of completing the course. Many landlords organised brake and charabanc trips for their regulars, generally to the seaside. South Shields was the usual venue for these trips, not only from Jarrow but the many pit villages in the area. More than one hundred were recorded one day as the horse drawn carriages trundled their way along the cobbled streets during the summer months for a picnic on the beach. Pictured here is the brake, heavy laden, outside the Golden Lion in the thirties.

The Bridge Inn was behind St. Paul's Church and owned by the McCagney family. Folklore has it that it was home to an animal half cat and half rabbit. The Bridge Inn is visible on the left of this photograph taken in the 1920s.

Not so very far from here was one of the busiest houses in Jarrow, the East Ferry Inn at Quay Corner, known for some reason as the 'Spike'. It became host to seafaring men of every nationality when Jarrow was a busy oil terminal, when 2/6d (12½p) would buy three bottles of Newcastle Brown Ale, five Woodbines, a box of matches and still leave 2d change. This picture was taken in 1940.

Church Bank and the river Don to the right of this photograph – another taken by James Hunter Carr in 1950. In the background is Bede Trading Estate which was opened in 1946, so large in its day it stretched into the Borough of South Shields. Beyond that is the municipal housing estate of Low Simonside.

The town's first **Ambulance Service** in 1918. This photograph was taken in the playground of the Ellison School where the ambulance and fire engines were garaged.

Copies of many of the photographs reproduced in this book can be obtained direct from the author, Paul Perry. (Telephone 091-489 6867).

Local titles published by S. B. Publications

Newcastle upon Tyne, Volumes 1 & 2
A Message from Sunderland

Other local areas: Merseyside, Greater Manchester, North Wales, Shropshire, Staffordshire, Cheshire, West Midlands, East Anglia, Hertfordshire, North London and Sussex

For full details: Write (enclosing S.A.E.) to S. B. Publications, Unit 2, Old Station Yard, Pipe Gate, Market Drayton, Shropshire. TF9 4AY.